What a Thing to
Say to the Queen!

What a Thing to Say to the Queen!

Charming Anecdotes from the House of Windsor

THOMAS BLAIKIE is the Manners and Etiquette Correspondent of *The Lady* magazine. He is the author of two previous best-selling books of Royal anecdotes, *You Look Awfully Like the Queen* and *Corgi and Bess*. He is also the author of *Blaikie's Guide to Modern Manners*. He lives in London.

Aurum

Brimming with creative inspiration, how-to
projects, and useful information to enrich your
everyday life, quarto.com is a favourite destination
for those pursuing their interests and passions.

First Published in 2015.

This edition published in 2022 by Aurum Press Ltd
an imprint of The Quarto Group
One Triptych Place,
London, SE1 9SH,
United Kingdom
T (0)20 7700 6700
www.quarto.com

A catalogue record for this book is
available from the British Library.

ISBN 978-0-7112-8599-6
Ebook ISBN 978-1-78131-481-4

1 3 5 7 9 10 8 6 4 2
2022, 2024, 2026, 2025, 2023

Typeset in Golden Cockerel ITC by
SX Composing DTP, Rayleigh , Essex

Printed and bound in Great Britain by
CPI Group (UK) Ltd, Croydon, CR0 4YY

Contents

Foreword

As the longest reigning monarch of this realm, the Queen embodied stability, hope and continuity. We loved her because she was always there, didn't make a fuss and was dedicated in her duty even in old age. But she adapted and the monarchy changed without appearing to do so. The Queen sent her first tweet in October 2014. Famously she played herself in a mini-Bond movie to mark the opening of the London 2012 Olympics and she delighted audiences around the world when she invited Paddington Bear for a cup of tea to celebrate her Platinum Jubilee in June 2022. She referred publicly to 'William and Kate' like everyone else; no stuffiness – not 'the Duke and Duchess of Cambridge'.

The strength of the behind-the-scenes vignettes and anecdotes you will find in this book springs from her outstanding personality and those of her immediate family, who between them have been at the heart of the royal scene for almost a hundred years.

The Queen was witty and quick, friendly and unstuffy, yet magically regal and formidable at the same time.

You'll see the Queen at home, even in the kitchen, then on official business, travelling and in the paddock at the races. Her eye for detail, her quick wit, her sensitivity, her unflappability and her modesty all shine through these stories, however small. Her mother and sister, too, emerge as exceptional personalities. While alive, Princess Margaret gave concern and could be impossible. But now she seems splendid, rather like the Queen in *Alice's Adventures in Wonderland*. The Queen Mother, too, was remarkable for her energy and the iron will with which she remained poised and charming for more than a hundred years. She was much cleverer and better informed than she let on and a tremendous life force.

We have much to celebrate in our Royal Family and I hope that this book suitably rises to the occasion and commemorates the late Queen as the longest-reigning monarch.

No Airs
and Graces

At Highclere, better known as Downton Abbey, a farm worker was wedged under a broken-down trailer when he heard a familiar voice asking, 'Can I help?' It was the Queen, in a headscarf, out walking with a dog. She is one of those guests who wants to make a contribution.

The Queen had an adventure getting to a private party in London recently. 'We were coming across the Park,' she told friends, 'when a policemen stepped in front of the car and made us wait while a big procession of vehicles passed by with blue flashing lights. It must have been a very important ruler.'

On the morning of 7 July 1983, the Queen awoke to find a stranger in her bedroom, wielding a shard of broken glass. The situation required patience as well as courage. 'Luckily I'm used to talking to people on street corners,' she said afterwards.

In October 1957, when the Queen, still in tiara and evening dress, left New York late at night after a ball, bystanders in their nightclothes lined the route to the airport, some of the women in curlers. 'I wouldn't stand out of doors in my dressing gown to see someone come by in a car, whoever they were,' the Queen remarked.

In the royal tea tent at Buckingham Palace garden parties, the Queen would take off her shoes, rest her hand on her hip and banter with her butler before resuming her rounds.

It was a big adventure meeting the Beatles at the Royal Variety Show in 1963. The Queen asked where their next show was. 'Slough, Ma'am,' Paul McCartney replied. She was delighted. 'Oh, that's near us!'

The estate of Princess Alice, mother of the Duke of Edinburgh, who died in December 1969, amounted to just three dressing gowns.

The Queen told Annie Leibovitz about the visit of a very different kind of photographer. 'Jane Bown came all by herself and I helped her move the furniture,' the Queen explained.

Camilla couldn't see what all the fuss was about over her forthcoming wedding to Prince Charles. 'It's just two old people getting hitched,' she remarked.

In 2000, Alan Titchmarsh was about to address the AGM of the Sandringham Women's Institute, by tradition held every January and chaired by the Queen. But he realised that Her Majesty was sitting awkwardly close, just on the other side of a trestle table. 'You push, and I'll pull,' she suggested. Thus they moved the table.

Elizabeth didn't truly feel a Queen until she saw the Windsor milk bottles emblazoned with E.R.

In the late 1950s, the Queen flew out to Corsica and Sardinia, but it rained. She went with Princess Alexandra to eat in simple local restaurants.

In 1959, the Queen was asked if she would meet an old lady of 105 who was waiting in her car. 'They shouldn't have done it. They might have killed her,' she said.

Her lady-in-waiting once remarked to the Queen, 'It's such thrill to do this.' They were driving right across the middle of Hyde Park Corner, a privilege only allowed to royalty. 'Oh, but it's so conspicuous,' said the Queen.

'The Queen will be here at teatime,' a courtier once told a young Prince Harry at Sandringham. 'Who's the Queen?' he enquired.

After church at Windsor on Sunday mornings, the Queen would invariably call on the Queen Mother at Royal Lodge, always slipping in the back way to avoid upstaging her.

At one of her favourite fashion houses, the Duchess of Cambridge needed to borrow suitable footwear for the dress she was trying on. All that could be found were white satin wedding shoes. The Duchess was delighted by the bizarre effect of black tights with white satin wedding shoes.

On most mornings, Princess Elizabeth, when living at Clarence House, walked her corgis in St James's Park, disguised in an old mac and headscarf.

A particularly dilapidated Rover was regularly seen on the Chelsea Embankment on Friday afternoons in the 1960s. The headscarved figure at the wheel was the Queen, driving herself down to Windsor for the weekend.

Once, when in Scotland, the Queen Mother shared her picnic with some random walkers she came across.

Lady Mountbatten often found people in need in the street and sent them down to her basement kitchen to be given a hot drink by her butler.

During his engagement, Prince Philip stayed at Kensington Palace with his grandmother, the Dowager Marchioness of Milford Haven. But the accommodation was derelict, with no carpets. The stairs creaked chronically and the Prince had to climb in via the roof to avoid waking his grandmother when returning after hours.

In the 1950s, the Duke of Edinburgh visited the Ideal Home Exhibition and the like. He would always come back with tins of soup, a washing machine or a food mixer – very welcome to 'a servantless couple in a small flat', according to his valet.

At the Royal Albert Hall in 1996, even Nelson Mandela was uncertain if he should get up and dance in the royal box as Ladysmith Black Mambazo began to play. But soon the Queen was on her feet and swaying, so it was all right.

The Life of State –
Not Always as
Expected

The Queen's head on British currency was not changed often, but other countries where she was head of state were more restless. The Sovereign was often asked to pick a profile of herself from a selection. A previous governor of the Bank of England, Mark Carney, confirmed that she always chose the least flattering one.

The Secretary of State for Northern Ireland in the Blair administration was rather astonished when his private meeting with the Queen (on a visit to the province) was interrupted by a maid announcing, 'Your bath is drawn, Ma'am.' The Queen bathed twice a day.

If the Queen ever looked just a little dour in public, there might have been a reason for it. At the rehearsal of the investiture of the Prince of Wales at Caernarfon in 1969, the crown was too big and, in the words of Noël Coward, 'extinguished him like a candlesnuffer'.

When it came to the real thing, the Queen struggled not to giggle.

The Queen was several times observed as she prepared to launch forth on engagements. A member of the press once glimpsed her behind a curtain, preparing to disembark from an aeroplane, standing absolutely still like a statute. In America in 1991 she was observed doing the same thing before leaving her guest quarters for the day.

'I know why you're here,' the Queen said to Malcolm Ross as they were both about to set out on horseback for Trooping the Colour. 'You're the one to get shot, not me.'

When the Queen recorded her Christmas broadcast, the producer put surprise silly pictures at strategic points to ensure that she smiled.

Once the Queen had got her heavy crown on, she was keen to get on with the State Opening of Parliament, but others were not always ready. She was cunningly prevented from leaving the Robing Room early, for instance, by the sudden appearance of a little travelling exhibition about the deteriorating state of the Palace of the Westminster. Each time they thought of something different.

'I'm glad the Emperor couldn't understand English,' the Queen said in October 1969. She had just driven up the Mall with him at the beginning of his state visit and had heard all too clearly the hostile comments from the crowd. The Emperor was of Japan.

The Queen began her speech to the Knights of the Garter at Windsor but stopped almost at once. 'I can't read this,' she declared. Was there something wrong with it? No, she'd forgotten her glasses and there was a pause while they were fetched.

'Oh dear, I wonder who's missing this?' Tidying up in the Robing Room at the House of Lords after the State Opening of Parliament once, the Queen found a rubber band on the floor. She held it up to general view but there were no claimants.

After their father became King, legal experts pored over the Act of Settlement and wondered whether, since there is no law of primogeniture amongst females, Elizabeth and Margaret would not share the throne when the time came.

When President Lebrun of France arrived for George VI's Coronation in 1937, little Princess Elizabeth was pushed forward to make a carefully prepared speech of welcome in French. There was consternation when the president subsequently addressed her. Would she collapse if required to speak spontaneously? She didn't, but engagingly explained her preparations for the occasion.

Princess Elizabeth was anxious for her sister before her father's coronation. 'I do hope she won't disgrace us by falling asleep in the middle. After all she is very young for a coronation.'

The Queen was about to leave for a state visit to Ghana in 1961 when a bomb blew up near the dias she was to occupy with President Nkrumah a few days later. But she would not cancel: 'How silly I should look if I were scared to visit Ghana and then Mr Khrushchev went a few weeks later.'

Visiting India in 1961, the Queen was amused by the vigorous enthusiasm of the crowds and the 'deadpan expression of their bullocks standing behind them'.

At the wedding of 'Stoker' Hartington, the Duke of Devonshire, the Queen looked downcast and preoccupied. 'Oh, I really must snap out of this and look smiley!' she said, 'I've had a whole morning full of problems.'

Lucy Worsley, Chief Curater at Historic Royal Palaces and TV presenter, reveals the existence of a photograph of Princess Margaret holding up a cushion on which is embroidered: 'It's Not Easy Being a Princess'

At the Great Children's Party in 1979, the biggest children's party ever in Hyde Park, the Queen and the Duke of Edinburgh toured the site standing up in the back of a Land Rover. But at one point, owing to an error of planning, the only onlookers were some ladies queuing for the loos. The Duke of Edinburgh gave a jolly wave. They were appalled.

When Queen Mary went to launch the liner SS *Queen Mary*, she said to her lady-in-waiting, 'Oh dear. I'm sure I'm not going to remember the name.'

In the 1980s, visiting the offices of *The Times*, the Queen discussed the miners' strike with Paul Routledge, the Labour editor. 'It's all about one man, isn't it?' she said. He didn't agree, telling her it was unlikely that one man could have kept 100,000 men out on strike for an entire year. But later Routledge became more greatly acquainted with Arthur Scargill through writing a biography of him. 'I feel I now owe the Queen an apology. By that stage, at any rate, the strike was about one man. Scargill may not have started the strike, but one word, one signal from him could have called it off before the struggle plumbed the depths of misery, violence and failure to which it sank... The Queen was right.'

The Royal Family was taking tea on the high terrace at Windsor during the last part of the Second World War when suddenly American voices were heard way below. 'Oh Lord, it's General Eisenhower. I forgot he was being shown round,' the King said. From their position they could not have communicated with this important person but he would have seen them. Perhaps also they should have invited him to tea. There was no hope but to hide under the table, which shook with royal giggles until the general had passed by. Luckily he did not notice.

Tony Blair launched 'Cool Britannia' early in his premiership. 'Poor Britannia, she'd have hated being cool,' the Queen Mother remarked.

Prince Harry persuaded the Queen to allow the ska band Madness to perform from the roof of Buckingham Palace at the Diamond Jubilee Concert. Officials had not been keen.

'I'll see what Harry says.' The courtier proposing the James Bond stunt for the opening ceremony of the Olympic Games had expected the Queen to be outraged. Harry was all for it.

George VI grew boisterous when finally his official duties were over. On the Royal Train in South Africa once he flung open the door of a lady's compartment where a fur was hanging. 'By God, some woman's left her beard in there,' he said.

As the Queen was setting out for Canada where she would open the Expo 67 Exhibition, Richard Crossman commiserated with her about the ghastliness of the displays. 'I'm too small to see them,' the Queen said.

The coronation tour of the East End of London was a tremendous success. When the Queen and the Duke of Edinburgh returned to Buckingham Palace they were buried in flowers to the extent that they could not get out of their open-top car.

The Duchess of Cornwall exited the tenth anniversary party of the Press Complaints Commission at Somerset House in February 2001 and got into her car. But where was her son, Tom Parker Bowles, who was supposed to be her escort? She couldn't just sit there so she opened the window and started chatting to a woman on the pavement. 'I'm waiting for my son,' she explained. 'He'll probably be ages. Chatting up girls I should think.'

The Prince's Trust Foundation dinner in 2000 was attended by Lauren Bacall and David Coulthard. But dear old Alan Whicker had no obvious connection. Why was he there? It turned out his wife, Valerie Kleeman, had been in the same lacrosse team as Camilla Parker Bowles (as she then was) at Queen's Gate School.

In 1989, the Queen delivered her Christmas broadcast from the stage of the Royal Albert Hall as part of the Save the Children Fund's Christmas concert. Right behind her a small child was nearly defeated by his enormous yellow flag which wavered dangerously in the Queen's direction as she was speaking. Just in time, a larger person intervened and got the flag upright again. 'I thought I was going to get hit,' the Queen said afterwards. Never work with children or animals.

'At Sandringham I feel a great deal more remote from London than at Balmoral,' the Queen told Richard Crossman, leader of the House of Commons, in January 1967.

Before the opening of the Severn Bridge in September 1966 the Queen was shown a model of the Almondsbury interchange of the M4 and M5 motorways. Nearby was a psychiatric home, the official explained, but the road would be completely hidden from it. 'They'll need that home,' the Queen remarked, 'to accommodate the people who go mad trying to find their way through this.'

In Trinidad in February 1965 there was no carriage to take the Queen to the State Opening of Parliament. She had to walk, in a state dress with, owing to the effects of sunburn, 'Monday's neckline not matching today's', according to Ann Leslie of the

Daily Express. In the parliament building a light bulb exploded with unusual violence.

After the Queen had tea and home-made fruit cake in the council house of Billy and Lucy Llewellyn in Newton Aycliffe, County Durham in 1960, Lucy said, 'I was thinking, such a weight on such a small pair of shoulders.'

The Queen was practising at home for the State Opening of Parliament, mainly for the benefit of the pages who carry her train. Suddenly the Imperial State Crown fell off. 'Oh dear,' she said, catching it deftly and putting it back on again.

In June 1977, the Queen arrived at the spot in Windsor Great Park where she was to light the first beacon of a chain that would span the country and thus launch the celebrations for her Silver Jubilee. Owing to huge crowds she was already late for the late-night event. 'Better hurry up,' said Major Mike Parker, the mastermind behind the would-be spectacular event. Rounding a corner, he saw that the 1948 London Olympic Torch with which the Queen was to light the beacon had gone out. 'Better slow down,' he said. 'Do make up your mind,' the Queen said. Finally the torch was lit, but the little boy designated to hand it to her burst into tears. 'You should be in bed,' the Queen told him. She lit the torch and watched the fuse burn happily towards the beacon, which mysteriously burst prematurely into flames. 'I can't think why you bothered asking me,' the Queen remarked. Then there was the most tremendous bang overhead. 'What on earth was that?' the Queen enquired. Mike Parker had no choice but to confess. 'Your Majesty,' he said, 'I'm afraid it's all gone terribly wrong.' There was an agonising frozen moment lasting apparently forever. Then the Queen said, 'Oh good. What fun!'

With the Truly Powerful

'That's pretty cool,' the Duke of Edinburgh remarked to Barbara Castle on seeing her name on the commemorative plaque at the opening of the Severn Bridge in September 1966. 'It was practically finished before you came along.' 'Not a bit of it,' she replied. 'It's entirely due to me that it was finished five months ahead of schedule. Anyway, I intend to be in on the act.' Barbara Castle said that she always argued with the Duke like mad and enjoyed his 'utter lack of stuffiness'.

In 1961, socialist MP Geoffrey de Freitas, who had been appointed high commissioner in Ghana, was dismissive of the protocol involved. Arriving at the palace, he said, 'What's all this about kissing hands? How long is it going to take?' But his meeting with the Queen over ran. Emerging, he said, 'That's astonishing! I've found out more about Ghana in the last half hour than I have in three weeks going round Whitehall.'

With her minsters not able to get home in time after the Privy Council meeting on Sunday 19 November 1967 to watch Harold Wilson's earth-shattering announcement on TV that he was devaluing the pound, the Queen had no choice but to offer her own set in her private sitting room. They watched together, but Richard Crossman was acutely aware of the awkward situation. What could the Queen say at the end that wasn't political? Even saying nothing might appear political. The Queen had a crafty solution: 'Of course it's extraordinarily difficult to make that kind of speech.' But Patrick Gordon Walker spoilt it by bellowing, 'Oh a wonderful performance.' Crossman changed the subject to foot-and-mouth disease.

When Churchill resigned as Prime Minister, the Queen planned to offer him a dukedom. The complication was that she did not wish him to accept because the palace was hoping to veer away from hereditary titles, especially dukedoms. Discreet enquires behind the scenes were made before the final audience and word came back that Sir Winston would surely wish to remain a commoner. However, in his own account, he revealed that, standing before his sovereign with whom he was besotted, he was suddenly inclined to accept. There was a nasty pause. When at last he said 'No', he could not understand why the Queen looked almost relieved.

At his first audience with the Queen, Harold Wilson was humiliated. She knew exactly what was in the Cabinet papers, but he hadn't a clue. Thereafter, he let her private secretary know beforehand what he intended to discuss with her.

In 1967, the Queen's private secretary explained to Richard Crossman that if he really didn't want to go to the State Opening of Parliament he could write to the Queen asking to be excused. Of course, Michael Adeane explained, she might wonder why she couldn't be excused, too, since she also disliked official ceremonies. Crossman went straight home and wrote to say he was coming.

King Abdullah of Saudi Arabia died in January 2015. It emerged that, in September 1998, he had visited Balmoral when he was Crown Prince, but in effect ruler because his older brother had had a stroke. After lunch the Queen offered him a drive round the estate. What he hadn't realised was that she would be at the wheel. In his own country, women, of whatever rank, weren't allowed to drive. He could scarcely run from the vehicle though, so they set off – at a devastating lick. Roaring around bends, Her Majesty talking all the time, the Crown Prince became frantic and begged through an interpreter that she slow down and look at the road. Some time later, the Saudi foreign minister said, 'I'm sure she steers the ship of state more steadily than she drives a Land Rover.' Diplomatic.

At the opening of the Severn Bridge in September 1966, Barbara Castle found it hard to conduct herself correctly as the National Anthem was being played because the Duke of Edinburgh was muttering sideways at her: 'When are you going to finish the M4. You've been a long time at it.'

President and Mrs George Bush Sr remained friends with the Queen since leaving office and sometimes saw her if they visited London. On one occasion, the former President picked up a small, three-legged silver dish of unusual shape and asked the Queen what it was for. She replied: 'I was hoping you could tell me. You gave it to me.'

Tony Benn asked the Queen her opinion of Pierre Trudeau, a long-haired fashion plate who happened to be the Prime Minister of Canada in the 1960s and 1970s. 'Rather disappointing,' was the Queen's view.

'You *can't* cancel Concorde,' the Queen told Tony Benn. Prince Charles, on a later occasion, followed up saying, 'You can't very well cancel Concorde now, can you?'

Two years in a row, Margaret Thatcher, famed for her super-human energy, had to sit down at the Buckingham Palace diplomatic reception. But the Queen remained standing. 'She's keeled over again!' she confided wickedly to her Archbishop of Canterbury.

In November 1999, Robin Cook, then the foreign secretary, was sitting in the Club World section of a British Airways aircraft making its way to South Africa. Suddenly a steward appeared from the first-class section, where a greater person was lodged, about to make a state visit. He bore a silver salver on which was a copy of the *Racing Post*. 'Her Majesty thought that the foreign secretary might be interested in seeing this,' he said. The Queen was one of the few who knew that he had once had a racing column in the *Glasgow Herald*.

In 1967, the Queen asked Richard Crossman how the new morning sittings of the House of Commons were going. His face betrayed irritation because there had been much sarcastic comment in the press about the shock to MPs of having to work in the mornings. At once the Queen said, 'Oh I'm sorry. I wasn't really criticising.' Crossman remarked, 'How sensitive she is.'

Not Quite How We Should be Treated

'What do you do?' a guest inquired of the Queen upon being introduced at a Buckingham Palace garden party in 2007. 'I had no idea what to say,' the Queen told friends afterwards.

'Lovely to have Windsor back again,' said the Queen at the party to mark the restoration of Windsor Castle after the terrible fire of 1992. A carpenter who had worked on the project was thrilled too, and twice dragged her away to meet his brothers. The Queen was amused by this unusual approach. Her only fear was that he might have twelve brothers.

A young boxer, Eddie Daniel from the Cook Islands, spied a vacant seat beside the Queen when she lunched in the athletes' canteen at the Commonwealth Games on her visit to Australia in March 2006. He decided to show his respect, so nipped in and kissed her on the cheek. She just smiled back. 'She is so cool, man,' he said.

When first married, the Queen Mother had nowhere to live. They tried White Lodge in Richmond Park but it was too far out. 'It would be very nice if we could live in the Queen's Dolls' House,' she remarked.

During the Second World War, owing to paper rationing, Princess Margaret often got cut out of newspaper photographs of the Royal Family. Lilibet wanted a round robin to editors: 'Please do not cut Princess Margaret out of pictures.'

Mike Parker, deviser of the afternoon party in the Mall for the Queen's golden jubilee, had an argument with Her Majesty a year or so beforehand about the gold coach. 'I'm not going to St Paul's in it,' the Queen told him. 'But you must,' said Mike Parker. 'No,' said the Queen. 'But why?' It turned out that the kind of clothes required for the gold coach would not be suitable for the afternoon party. 'But you could always change during the lunch stopover at the Guildhall,' Mike Parker informed the Queen. The next day her private secretary was fuming down the line. 'What on earth do you think you're doing suggesting such a thing to the Queen?' But she did go in the gold coach and she did change her clothes – driving out in blue and emerging from Guildhall after lunch in red.

Right after Christmas 1988, president-elect Bush wanted to announce whom he was appointing as ambassador in London. 'You can't,' they said. 'You've got to wait until the host country accepts the appointment.' 'Too bad,' he said. 'I've got my party to think of.' So the Queen had to get on with it right away and fax her approval from Sandringham overnight.

Lady Airlie gave Princess Elizabeth a dustpan and brush for Christmas in 1928.

At Windlesham Moor, where she lived in the 1940s, Princess Elizabeth had to scurry around fetching stray balls from the rhododendrons during her husband's impromptu cricket matches.

Danny Kaye visited Windlesham Moor and on his departure curtsied profoundly to the Princess.

In the early 1950s, Princess Elizabeth was in America. President Truman took her to see his bedridden elderly mother-in-law, Mrs Wallace. 'I've brought Princess Elizabeth to see you,' he yelled at her. 'I'm so glad your father has been re-elected, ' the ancient lady replied. In fact it was Churchill who had been re-elected.

George VI's coffin rested in a passageway for seventeen years before a vault could be built for it in 1969.

England's premier baron, Lord Mowbray, Segrave and Stourton, made an impact as he approached to pay homage at the Queen's coronation. 'There were mothballs and pieces of ermine flying all over the place,' the Queen said later. He also had filthy hands.

Given the task of registering the Queen Mother's death, Margaret Rhodes, her niece, was asked by the registrar: 'What was the husband's occupation?' 'King,' she replied.

Bring your own sideboard and stand on it! This was the approach of one family determined to get a view of the honeymooning Princess Elizabeth as she attended Sunday service at Romsey Abbey in November 1947.

What was more terrifying – enemy bombers overhead or Lady Reading, head of the WVS? When bombs began to fall during a meeting with this indomitable figure at Buckingham Palace during the Second World War, the Queen (later, Queen Mother) would have liked to suggest moving away from the windows and the risk of broken glass but did not dare.

The Resident Factor grimaced as he rose to greet the Queen at the Ghillies Ball at Balmoral. His bare legs had stuck to the leather banquette on which he had been sitting. He was not trouserless but wearing a kilt.

Preparing to go out of the palace (or 'house', as she calls it), into the seething streets on VE night, Princess Elizabeth pulled down her ATS cap as much as possible for disguise. But a grenadier in the group wouldn't have anyone incorrectly dressed in his presence, so she had to put it on properly.

A tree planted by the Duke of Windsor, while King, at Adsdean, then the Mountbatten's country place, never flourished and died soon after the end of his ten-month reign.

In 1938, the Windsors in exile found temporary refuge at 24 Boulevard Suchet, Paris. Their view was of soldiers washing in the barrack yard next door.

After engagements in the Midlands in the 1940s, Princess Elizabeth and the Duke of Edinburgh stayed overnight in a country house with no plumbing. The lady of the house had ordered grass cuttings to be heaped in the hall before being conveyed to the kitchen 'to help the food situation'.

In the early days, the innovative Duke of Edinburgh liked to fly whenever possible. But when bad weather prevented his flight to Edinburgh, he was stranded at Grantham and had to barge on to a crowded train instead. A young mother wielding a potty was horrified when she saw who it was.

The boys at Gordonstoun ran a racket selling off items belonging to Prince Charles. Name tags went for half a crown but his actual signature would fetch five shillings.

In about 2011, the stud manager at Bushy Park asked a driver to move his lorry because he was expecting an important visitor; but still the Queen arrived to find a pantechnicon in her way. 'I didn't realise quite how important,' the driver explained.

Camilla, Duchess of Cornwall, once earned highly commended in a flower show near Birkhall. She'd picked the flowers herself. 'She did well for a first-time entrant,' the organiser said.

When Queen Wilhelmina arrived at Buckingham Palace during the Second World War, having got out of the Netherlands just in time as the Germans invaded, she was naturally preoccupied with security. 'What would happen,' she asked of George VI, 'if the Germans started parachuting into the garden right now?' 'Oh, I'll show you,' said the King nonchalantly and pressed a panic button. Whereupon absolutely nothing happened.

At Aintree one year for the Grand National, Richard Dimbleby unfortunately stumbled outside the BBC commentary box and became entangled in a way not quite usual with the Queen Mother who happened to be standing nearby. 'I didn't know you cared,' she remarked, letting him off the hook.

In his younger days, Prince Charles got away early from naval training and hurled off to Royal Ascot. He thought he'd wait by the gate and wave to his mother and her party as they passed in their landaus, but a security man tried to shoo him away. 'I needn't have waited anyway,' the Prince said. 'They all went by in the carriage and looked the other way.'

At Eton, the Queen Mother and her guests fell into the hands of schoolboys. Several times a term she would attend Sunday morning service at Eton Chapel but, because she was there in a private capacity, the provost of Eton could not meet her. All he could do was ensure that the boys knew how to mix her drinks and hope for the best.

Prince Charles took pity on a disconsolate girl by the wayside near Balmoral. She said she was lost so he gave her a lift to the main road. The following year, he saw another young woman in the same situation in the same place. Again he stopped. It was the same person. Fishy.

The Prince of Wales was paying a friendly visit to one of his tenants and asked to use the facilities. The host recalled too late the joke mug in the bathroom

showing his visitor with one of his supposedly stick-
ing-out ears as the handle.

The Queen drew up at the Royal Windsor Horse
Show in 1991 in a black Vauxhall Carlton. 'Sorry, love,
you can't come in without a sticker,' security man
Carl Shimmin, told her. 'I think if you check I will be
allowed to come in,' the Queen said, winding down
her window. 'I thought she was some old dear who
had got lost,' the guard remarked later.

As the Queen shook hands with the shot-put cham-
pion Geoff Capes at the Braemar Highland Games in
1982, the resin on his palms, used to improve grip,
caused him to adhere to his sovereign. Once unglued,
the Queen clapped her gloved hands together but,
too late, they were stuck. The Queen pulled grim
faces and there was much merriment amongst the
royal party.

The Queen once found herself, in an art gallery,
surrounded by large numbers of Lucian Freud's
somewhat uncompromising female nudes. 'Weren't
you painted by Lucian Freud?' the curator inquired
by way of conversation. 'Yes, but not like this,' the
Queen replied.

At a spectacular, staged at the Earls Court Exhibition
Centre, for the fortieth anniversary of the Queen's
accession in 1992, a group of children was supposed

to present the Queen with a newly commissioned Commonwealth Mace at a certain point. They stationed themselves before the Royal Box but did not hand over the mace. There was a bit of a face-off with the Queen standing for some time before the uncooperative children. At length the Queen said, 'Can I have the mace?' 'No,' the head child said, 'not until the music stops.'

Our Jewels
and Clothes

If the Imperial State Crown isn't available (i.e. it is on view to tourists at the Tower of London), the Queen practises for the State Opening of Parliament with a sack of flour on her head of equivalent weight.

Visiting Northern Ireland in May 2009, the Queen was coming down the stairs for dinner when she discovered she'd lost an earring. 'They were Mummy's,' she cried, casting about for the missing jewel. She was in quite a state. The Duke of Edinburgh carried on.

Norman Hartnell's sketches for the coronation dress included the emblems of England, Scotland, Ireland and Wales. In that case, said the Queen, what about those of all the dominions? Hartnell found that he had a lot more embroidery to do.

In November 1988, the Queen went to the Royal Albert Hall for the Wightman Cup, a team tennis

competition for women. Although it was a night-time event, she wore a day outfit suitable for a sporting occasion. But everybody else, because she was coming, was in full evening regalia. 'I felt a little underdressed,' she told an aide afterwards.

Bobo MacDonald, the Queen's dresser, who had been with her since childhood, found that no mirrors had been provided for the Queen and her maids of honour in the Robing Room at Westminster Abbey, which was in the specially built annexe by the west door. Steps were taken.

In 1952, for the Queen Mother, one of the many deprivations of no longer being Queen was lack of diamonds. She wrote to her daughter, the Queen, days before the Coronation, desperate to get hold of some. If she got no reply, she remarked, she'd have to root out some of Granny's. Would that be alright? In the event, the Queen Mother showed up at the Coronation wearing three diamond necklaces.

When Princess Diana was plainly winning the popularity war with her husband, the Queen Mother remarked, 'Let's face it. People aren't interested in seeing someone in the same suit every week.'

'I can't wear beige because people won't know who I am,' the Queen once said.

The Queen remarked of shoulder pads, popular in the 1980s: 'All right for Miss Collins, but not really for me.'

Her puffy cream evening dress, its meringue effect worsened by large bows at the shoulders, was much criticised on the Queen's state visit to America in the 1980s. Afterwards the Queen said, 'Oh, don't go on about it. I think it's a very pretty dress and I'm going to like it. Just take the bows off.'

Princess Margaret once commented on a pretty brooch the Queen was wearing. The Queen's response was vague, because she leaves jewellery to her dresser and often forgets what she has on. '*I* gave it to you,' said the nearby Queen Mother.

According to his valet, Prince Philip couldn't tie a tie and was quite capable of selecting suede shoes with evening dress.

Princess Margaret would always parade through the corridors in any new outfit to see 'how well it walked'.

Queen Mary, 'her old Grannie and subject', may have wished to be the first to curtsy to the new Queen on her sudden return from Kenya after her father, King George VI's, death. But the ancient Majesty had another purpose: 'Lilibet, your skirts are too short for mourning,' she pronounced.

The Queen Mother could not endure to be without her pearls. So if they needed to be restrung, she had to have them back the same day. The crown jeweller, David Thomas, found this a challenge.

In the privacy of Sandringham, the Prince of Wales thought to try out a new look at Christmas 2014. His monocle was met with derision from the family unfortunately.

Those calling on the newly arrived Princess Anne in 1950 were surprised by the dress code: a gauze face mask was required, owing to medical fashion at the time.

'What is that man wearing?' the Queen whispered to Prince Philip, peering down from the aircraft to the welcome party below on her arrival in Texas in 1991. Sherard Cowper-Coles, a member of the British diplomatic team, was so proud of his blue-and-white-striped seersucker suit, bought specially for the occasion. One of his colleagues had overheard the Queen's remark and passed it on. The suit was never seen again.

The Prince of Wales wore the insignia of a Dame Commander of the Order of the Nile at President Sadat of Egypt's funeral in 1981. Both he and Princess Diana had been awarded this order only a few weeks before by the President, but his valet had packed the wrong one

The Duchess of Cambridge has only one pair of gloves. So she revealed at the lunch in Westminster Hall for the Queen's Diamond Jubilee. And Prince William doesn't like them. They have cutout backs.

John Driscoll left Hartnell in the late 1950s to set up on his own. His premises were tiny – with just one sewing machine – in a side street in Eastbourne. But soon an important call came through. The Queen wanted him to make suits for country wear out of Balmoral tartan. His wife had to learn to type so the bills looked credible.

Barbara Castle complimented the Queen on her dress at the state banquet for President Frei of Chile in July 1965. The Queen was delighted, but Princess Margaret homed in on her order, pinned to her sister's breast. 'It's rather prominent, darling. Well, it does rather stick out.' 'It's all right for the men,' the Queen replied. 'They can wear it in their lapel but I have to pin it on somewhere.'

The Queen's handbag had an unusual secondary function – as a signalling device. Handbag placed on the dinner table means, 'I want to leave in five minutes.' Handbag moved from arm to arm says, 'It's time to talk to someone else.'

The Queen's handbag also contained good luck charms from her children, including miniature dogs and horses, and family photos.

The Queen wore her gold Blue Peter badge at the tea party she gave for the fiftieth anniversary of the children's programme in October 2008.

At the 2014 opening ceremony of the Commonwealth Games in Glasgow, the Queen applied her lipstick in full view of the crowd. Onlookers said 'It looks suspiciously like Clarins.'

Our Feminine
Allure

In 1972, Gough Whitlam became prime minister of Australia. He had Republican tendencies. The Queen wondered what to do about this, but when he visited her at Windsor bearing a gift of a huge sheepskin rug her path was clear. She lay on it and declared it lovely to stroke. Mr Whitlam later said that the Queen had a good pair of legs. No more was heard of an Australian republic – for a while at least.

After his wife, the actress Valerie Hobson, died, Jack Profumo told friends that he was inundated with offers from other women. 'Who exactly?' The Queen Mother apparently. She was one of the first to show up with an oven-ready lasagne for the helpless widower, as it were.

It is always said that Labour politicians are much more ferociously loyal to the monarchy than the Tory ones. Now perhaps we know why. Once, walking in the garden at Buckingham Palace with Jim Callaghan, the Queen picked a lily of the valley and placed it in his buttonhole.

Sir Charles Forte thought the Italian baritone in the line-up to meet the Queen at Covent Garden was a bit much with his lavish compliments and overt enthusiasm for Her Majesty's smile. The great hotelier tried to steer her away, but she was irresistibly drawn back to the charmer: 'You were saying…' she murmured. On another occasion the Queen was most excited when an Italian waiter gave her a red rose in Windsor high street.

Married Life

In 1940, Princess Elizabeth was keen to get Prince Philip on to Queen Mary's knitting list for wartime scarves. But he was serving in the tropics at the time.

'Philip?' The Queen sought her husband's attention and didn't get it. He was reading the sports section. It was 1957 and they were on board President Eisenhower's special aircraft, waiting for take off. 'Philip!' she tried again. 'In what order do they start the engines on a plane like this?' But Philip was puzzled. 'It's no use waiting until they actually start,' the Queen teased.

At the after party for Charles and Diana's wedding, Prince Philip refused to obey the Queen's command that he remove his party beanie provided by Lester Lanin's orchestra.

Arriving at St Paul's in March 2015 for the service to mark the end of Britain's involvement in the war in Afghanistan, the Duke of Edinburgh omitted to place his white gloves on the tray provided at the west door, as protocol requires. The Queen was not pleased. Finally, they encountered a familiar member of staff in the line-up; 'Give him your gloves,' she said firmly. 'Give him your gloves.'

In Nigeria during 2003, Labour MP Chris Mullin noticed that Prince Philip was getting huffy, because there was too much jargon in the speech at the opening of the British Council offices. 'Come and look…' said the Queen, gesturing generally into the distance, '…at the pottery'. Mullin went round afterwards but could see no pottery.

There were lots of parties on Malta in the 1940s, when Princess Elizabeth was enjoying a spell as an ordinary naval officer's wife. Spoons and buns would fly through the air, according to Henriette Abel Smith, the lady-in-waiting. If it got really hazardous, Prince Philip would sit both ladies on the piano to keep them out of danger.

A stand-in valet thought the Duke of Edinburgh's proper valet had forgotten to pack his pyjamas. This was at Menabilly, Daphne du Maurier's home in Cornwall. But the offer of a borrowed pair was rejected: 'Never wear the things.'

Prince Philip was relieving his frustration on the squash court at Buckingham Palace when *finally* his first child was born at 9.14 p.m. on 14 November 1948 in the same building.

Early in their marriage, Princess Elizabeth and the Duke of Edinburgh were in Rome on her birthday. She would have liked to have gone to a restaurant, but Philip organised a grand Embassy party. She didn't speak to him for several days.

If Prince Philip entered a room after the Queen, he apologised.

Lord Mountbatten was being driven across Windsor Home Park at great speed by the Duke of Edinburgh in a sports car. The Queen, in the front passenger seat, clung silently to the door handle but, when they hurtled round a bend practically on two wheels, her sharp intake of breath was heard by her husband. 'If you do that again, I'll put you out,' he barked. She made not a sound for the rest of the terrifying journey. At their destination, Mountbatten wondered why the Queen did not protest more. 'You heard what he said,' she explained.

'I'm sure Prince Philip is mad,' Princess Elizabeth confided in a member of staff. He was running with four sweaters on and then had to lie down.

At the Science Museum in 2014, the Queen sent her first tweet. On departure, she said the presents she had been given would be put in the Round Tower at Windsor. 'And mine, too.' The Duke of Edinburgh wasn't going to be left out.

At the launch of the *QE2* on Clydeside in September 1967, the Queen was overcome with emotion as the ship slid down the slipway; as was Princess Margaret. Fortunately the Duke of Edinburgh was on hand with a handkerchief. 'This is when a man has to become a mother,' he said

'Not a very good likeness, is it?' the Duke of Edinburgh commented as the Queen signed a photo mount at the launch of the cruise ship, *Britannia*, in March 2015. Where the photo should have been, there was nothing; it was blank, the image of Her Majesty to be inserted later.

Royal Dining

—✦—

No Amorini, heart-shaped chocolates coated in silver or bright colours, at the American Ambassador's dinner in 1963: the Queen's particular request while she was pregnant with Prince Edward.

Unfamiliar guests at lunch or dinner might be fooled by the Queen's napkins but she is always ready to explain: 'You've got to have the starched side up or else the thing will fall on the floor. You see over there. They've got it all wrong.'

'She stacked the plates!' the artist, George 'Frolic' Weymouth, complained after enjoying a buffet with the Queen at Windsor.

From the Castle of Mey, the Queen Mother sent an urgent message to her daughter the Queen on board *Britannia*: 'Grave shortage of lemons. Could you bring some?' This explains the plastic bag the Queen carried as she disembarked from the yacht.

Nancy Reagan was surprised to find that the route to the terrace where she had been invited to breakfast with the Queen at Windsor was through the royal bedroom. But the boxes of cereal stumped her completely. 'What do I do?' she asked Prince Charles, who said, 'Just help yourself.'

Dinner at President Reagan's Californian ranch was enchiladas, tacos and refried beans. 'That was so enjoyable,' the Queen remarked afterwards, 'especially the used beans.'

In San Francisco in 1983, the Queen was persuaded by Prince Philip to have dinner at Trader Vic's. 'I haven't been to a restaurant for fifteen years,' she said. The next year, on a private visit to Wyoming, she went to the Maverick Supper Club. The waitress reeled off the choice of salad dressings: 'Ya got French, Italian, ranch, honey, mustard or house.' As many of her subjects would have been, the Queen was totally at sea.

In June 2011, the Queen was having lunch at Windsor with racing friends. 'Boeing 747,' she said at one point. Then she said, 'Airbus'. The Castle is right next to Heathrow airport and planes roar overhead. The Queen knows them all by their sound.

Lady Pamela Mountbatten had been successfully dieting when the Queen asked her on the six-month coronation tour of 1953 as lady-in-waiting. 'You

can always choose the menus,' she said by way of enticement.

The Captain of the *Gothic* , the ship used for the coronation tour of 1954, said that the Queen enjoyed 'pottering about in the little pantry attached to her suite… Smith, her steward, could never get used to the fact that she so rarely rang for him.'

'If it was customary to have porridge at every meal,' Prince Philip once said, 'Lilibet would have it.'

Launching the new cruise ship *Britannia* in March 2015, the Queen told the TV chef James May that she saw white bread for the first time on board the old *Queen Elizabeth*. 'It was rather fascinating,' she added.

The Queen Mother liked to pick over her lunch parties with her page of the backstairs, William Tallon. Once she wondered aloud whether his partner, Reg Wilcox, who also worked at Clarence House, might not join in the discussion. 'It'll be like St Trinian's,' she said.

Sausage and mash was one of the little princesses' favourite dinners.

There have been no fish knives in royal palaces since Edward VII denounced them as 'very common'.

'Butter pats!' the Queen exclaimed in general conversation with a stallholder at the Sandringham show. 'There's something I really do know how to make.'

Royal catering tips include: placing the pudding spoon and fork above the table mat, which is considered 'restaurant'; all potatoes have to be the same size.

During the Second World War, Princesses Elizabeth and Margaret stayed at Windsor (what is a castle for, after all?), eating bottled plums from the garden every day for pudding.

As a child, Prince Harry was pleased to do his mother a favour and use a plastic tablecloth to save her the bother of getting a real one cleaned.

Diana took both her sons to San Lorenzo, her favourite Italian restaurant in Beauchamp Place, where there were no fish fingers, which disappointed Harry.

The Queen Mother drank raw milk every morning. Hence her long life, possibly.

The Queen Mother's maid often found chocolates with teeth marks in the wastepaper basket in her room. Her Majesty was devoted to chocs but not all centres were favoured.

Princess Elizabeth took bacon, eggs and tea for breakfast. In later years, the Queen had toast and marmalade, most of which was distributed amongst the corgis.

The Queen's favourite meal was afternoon tea.

The Duke of Edinburgh, struck down with jaundice in the 1950s, insisted he could eat fried eggs provided they were cooked with butter rather than oil, but his valet would only allow boiled eggs.

In the old days, even the smallest dinner at Buckingham Palace required one man from the glass pantry, another from the silver pantry and a third

from the china pantry just to lay the table. A footman brought the food from the kitchen and another waited at table, with a spare in case of errands. When the Queen and the Duke of Edinburgh took over, they went self-service.

If she was away for any length of time, the Queen Mother's menservants liked to dress up in her hats. Once she said to William Tallon, her page of the backstairs: 'I quite understand if you want to wear my hats and other things, but do try to put them back where you found them.'

The Queen's first meal as Queen was eaten on an aeroplane to Entebbe in Uganda. Venison, duck, ham, orange sauce, boiled eggs, salad, strawberries and cream were served.

Austerity was eagerly practiced at Buckingham Palace during the Second World War. But one day the Queen, later the Queen Mother, went too far in her wartime housekeeping. 'I don't know what's in these sandwiches,' the King said. 'Sawdust, I suppose.'

Sir Dingle Foot, at a formal dinner, was confused to suddenly find two partridges on his plate whereas before there had been only one. His neighbour was the culprit, it emerged. She didn't want her partridge and had deftly transferred it. She was also the guest of honour, the Queen Mother.

At her first proper married home, Princess Elizabeth's favourite dessert was pancakes with lemon and sugar. 'If we put them on the menu with something else, she'd always cross out the something else,' her footman, John Gibson recalls. Staff noticed a considerable increase in numbers for lunch on pancake days. It seemed the pancakes, made by Betty Herridge, the first kitchenmaid, were acquiring a reputation.

Prince Charles's nanny, Helen Lightbody, always phoned down to the kitchen at Clarence House to discuss His Royal Highness's lunch at the most awkward moment, just as the kitchen was about to serve the staff lunch. What's more, whatever had been prepared, she wanted the opposite. Eventually Betty Herridge got round this by offering, for example, chicken, mashed potato, carrots and peas, while actually having to hand liver and cabbage.

The Prince of Wales often catnaps at dinner parties. Hostesses in the know continue talking and nobody notices. Even two minutes 'out' will refresh him completely.

The Prince of Wales loathes chocolate pudding of any kind. A chocolate biscuit is alright but a pudding…and with nuts on it! Ugh!

'Why are there sixteen chickens in the freezer when I'm only here for three days?' the Prince of

Wales asked the chef at Highgrove. 'Well, Sir, you do like your vol-au-vents,' was the reply.

By Prince William's special request, a second cake made entirely of McVitie's chocolate biscuits was served at his wedding reception.

At Sandringham the kitchen is right next to the dining room. Once the Queen and Princess Margaret came in to look at the Christmas hamper which had arrived from Harrods, while the chef, Darren McGrady, was engaged in making two hundred pancakes, using a spatula to turn them. 'Isn't that cheating?' the Queen said. 'Aren't you supposed to toss them?' So that's what he did and the Queen and Princess Margaret loved the spectacle.

If a chef is offering to make a dish unknown to the Queen, she wants to see the recipe before giving the go-ahead.

A fanciful garnish, dreamt up by a chef formerly of Le Gavroche, involving a whole lemon to sit alongside the Queen's scrambled eggs with smoked salmon was returned untouched to the royal kitchen with a message: 'This is a waste.'

If the Queen and Princess Margaret had picked some berries in a hedgerow at Sandringham or Balmoral, they'd send them to the kitchen with instructions as to how they were to be served at dinner that day.

We Are Royal
After All

When Mary Soames, Churchill's youngest daughter, went to Buckingham Palace to receive the Order of the Garter, the Queen said, 'It's on your father's chain.' 'It can't be, Ma'am. That chain is in a glass case at Chartwell.' Lady Soames felt awful contradicting the Monarch. 'It was. But it isn't now,' said the Queen. Evidently she had been at work behind the scenes.

When the Queen Mother's friend Tortor Gilmour relocated to a smaller house, Her Majesty suggested a few improvements on her first visit: 'You must have them close that petrol station and move that school.'

In December 1981, the Queen summoned the Fleet Street editors to Buckingham Palace because Princess Diana couldn't stand any more media attention. 'But why doesn't she send a servant to buy sweets rather than go out herself?' Barry Askew, editor of the *News of the World*, asked helpfully. 'That, if I may say so, is a very pompous remark,' the Queen answered.

In 2007, the Queen hosted a reception for prominent Americans in London. She took an interest in
the callused hands of some rowers, and talked to
Brian McBride, a top player for Fulham, but somebody barged into the group. 'Do you play football,
too?' asked the Queen. 'No, I sell pancake and waffle
mix in the Middle East.' 'How interesting what people will eat,' the Queen said as she disappeared.

Princess Margaret's apartment in Kensington Palace
was cunningly numbered 1A to give a modest
impression. In fact, it contained a dog-washing room
and a room solely for the nurture of orchids, among
many other rooms.

'I've tried a remote control for my television,' the
Queen Mother said, 'but really it's so much easier to
ring.'

In 2008 the Queen and the Duke of Edinburgh went
to the London offices of Google where they encountered the dress-down style of the modern office.
'Just back from jogging?' the Duke asked marketing
executive, Matthew Trewhella, because of his
hoodie, trainers and chinos.

Edward VIII visited Royal Lodge, bringing for the
first time Mrs Simpson who looked calmly out of
the window and pronounced that some trees and
part of a hill might be moved for a better view.

The little princesses are often said to have had a limited education, but where art appreciation was concerned they had an advantage. One picture a week was brought from the Royal Collection and placed on an easel in their schoolroom. Lilibet's favourite was *Maidservant Cleaning Pan* by Gerard Dou, at 6in square, the smallest picture in the collection.

One attraction of Hill House at Knightsbridge as a junior school for Prince Charles, was that the pavement outside was scrubbed every day and the railings regularly dusted.

Princess Elizabeth thought 7s 6d too much to ask for a ticket to the wartime pantomime of Cinderella starring herself and her sister. 'No one will pay that to see us.' 'Nonsense. They'll pay anything,' said Princess Margaret.

It was Princess Margaret's job to find the six maids of honour to carry the Queen's train at the coronation. By precedent from the crowning of Queen Victoria they were to be all aged about twenty, unmarried, of similar dimensions and in rank at least an earl's daughter. 'We need quins and an extra,' said Princess Margaret.

Like many of us, Robert Fellowes had no idea there was anything wrong with his handwriting. But when he was fairly new as the Queen's private secretary, one of her correspondents wrote: 'I notice you have a new private secretary, a Mr Lehan.' The Queen reminded Robert Fellowes that he was not a doctor.

Martin Charteris, when he was the Queen's private secretary, once drafted a speech where she was to say, 'I'm very glad to be in Birmingham today.' The Queen crossed out the 'very'.

'Run him down!' So Princess Margaret ordered her chauffeur if ever she saw Tommy Lascelles, her elderly neighbour at Kensington Palace. As the Queen's private secretary at the time of the Townsend affair, he had ruined her life, she claimed.

'What presents have you got for us?' any child enquires when a parent returns from afar. In 1927, in the case of the little princesses, the answer was: three tons of toys from the people of New Zealand and Australia. But they were given away of course.

There was a certain agreeable logic in Queen Mary's approval of Catherine the Great: it was out of love for her kingdom that she committed terrible crimes.

Prince Charles's pram was washed thoroughly every-day, with particular attention to the wheels and tyres.

On *Britannia*, the floor level of the Queen and Philip's cabin was 2ft higher than the deck outside so those passing by couldn't see in.

Once the intruder, Michael Fagan, had been removed from her bedroom early in the morning of 9 July 1982, the Queen got back into bed to have her tea as planned.

'I'm the biggest "P" for Princess,' announced Princess Elizabeth as she squabbled with her cousin over

ownership of a wooden bench at Birkhall during the Second World War. The Queen Mother was known to her family as 'Peter' but was never, officially at least, a Princess.

Denys Rhodes, husband of the Queen Mother's niece, Margaret Rhodes, was complaining one day at Balmoral that he badly needed a title for his latest book. 'And I cannot think of a reason for giving you one,' an unexpected voice suddenly said at the back of the room. The Queen had entered unseen.

The Queen was anxious for her mother in her advanced age and gave her a walking stick. The Queen Mother used it grudgingly and once, at the end of an engagement, flung it dismissively into the back of her car.

'Wireless!' Princess Margaret would yell from the back of her car. Accordingly the radio was switched on.

Even the Queen, later Queen Mother, curtsied to Queen Mary when she left Sandringham by car.

'Where is the Princess?' Prince Charles, aged three, enquired on coming in from the garden at Buckingham Palace. He meant his own mother. He was told she had gone out. 'But why? She knew I was coming back.'

Princess Margaret went unannounced to a humble oyster bar in Galway. At one point she muttered something to her husband who muttered to someone else who in turn muttered to another. Finally the proprietor was made to understand that the Princess was uncomfortable. It took five people four minutes to scour the facility from top to bottom.

The Queen's 86th birthday treat was first of all Newbury Races, then Gary Barlow. She went back to Sydmonton, Andrew Lloyd Webber's country house, where the Take That star sang a special version of 'Happy Birthday' to her.

In the early part of the Second World War, Lord Halifax, taking a shortcut through the Buckingham Palace gardens for some reason, came under fire from the Queen, later Queen Mother, and her ladies. They were practising self-defence in the event of a kidnap attempt by the enemy.

In Saudi Arabia, on an official visit, Prince Charles wanted a no-frills chance to paint in the desert. So he was taken to a lonely sand dune and left in a traditional tent with carpet walls. But, tucked away out of sight, to back up the primitive tent, was a sea of vehicles providing hot and cold running water, a mobile hospital, a mobile phone mast, electricity generators and Wi-Fi service.

There were no commemorative tea towels for the wedding of Prince William and Kate Middleton. Official photographs and the Prince's coat of arms were also banned from T-shirts and aprons.

Visiting the Valleys Kids Soar Centre in South Wales in 2008, Prince William was challenged to a game on a Wii games console by eighteen-year-old Martyn James. 'I never thought I'd be playing Wii on an official engagement,' the Prince said, adding a word of warning to his opponent. 'You know you're not allowed to beat me.' Later Martyn James attributed his defeat to nerves.

'I knew things were getting serious when I found a helicopter in my garden,' Michael Middleton explained in his father-of-the-bride speech at his daughter's wedding.

'I suppose we ought to permeate,' Princess Margaret said to her sister the Queen after a state banquet when they had been some time in the drawing room.

Staff

The Queen was very insistent that Paul Whybrew, her sergeant-at-arms and most trusted personal servant, be given a Thames-side home *for life*.

Informed that St Mary's Wantage was merging with Heathfield School at Ascot and that the Wantage site was to close, the Queen was astonished. 'Most of my ladies-in-waiting went there,' she protested.

Why did the Queen suddenly cry 'Hurrah!' as she drove a guest around the Balmoral estate? She'd seen one of her gamekeepers strolling with a young woman. Previously the man's wife had left him so this was an encouraging development.

'I'm as nervous as you are,' the Queen reassured her ear, nose and throat specialist, Sir Cecil Hogg, as he attempted to examine her.

Sir Robert Fellowes, the Queen's one-time private secretary, messed up one day. The schedule was so crowded that his mistress had to miss her hair appointment. 'I'll have to think about employing a woman,' she said.

When Fellowes, who was Princess Diana's brother-in-law, was appointed private secretary, she said, 'It's the first time I've got a private secretary I held in my arms as a baby.'

The Queen granted fifteen sittings to the artist Lucian Freud between May 2000 and December 2001, not in the usual grand palace drawing room but in an art restoration studio in St James's Palace. He wanted the Queen in the royal diadem but with a blue day suit, not the usual state dress. The finished portrait was disliked by many who were unfamiliar with the artist's approach. Because of the value of the diadem, protection officers had to be present, but Freud found them distracting and the Queen asked them to go outside. One of the men, the Queen said, she knew quite well. While picking up birds at a shoot on a friend's estate, a cock pheasant had hurtled out of a hedge and knocked her over. There was blood. The officer rushed up and, hurling himself upon her, began administering the kiss of life. He thought she'd been shot. The Queen was impressed and engaged him in her own protection squad.

Princess Elizabeth had to seek the advice of her steward in her first married home at Windlesham Moor. If her father was coming to dinner, should he be seated, as King, at the head of the table, or as a guest at the side? The steward explained that in a private residence the King could be a guest. 'You were quite right,' the Princess told him afterwards. 'The King said nothing about the placing.'

If any of the Queen Mother's staff suggested that, approaching eighty, they might retire, she would simply say, 'Congratulations. You'll feel marvellous in your eighties.' At least she spoke with some authority, for she took this line when herself over ninety.

In 1975, Sir Hugh Casson redesigned the Royal Train. Bobo MacDonald, had very particular requirements. 'Bobo was the client really,' Casson remarked.

In the old days at Sandringham, Christmas presents were given to servants after the King's Christmas broadcast. Medals were worn and women and girls had white gloves. A charwoman said to the Queen Mother, then Queen, 'You're the sort of person I'd like to have as a neighbour,' which she considered one of the nicest compliments ever paid her.

His valet and footman held up cards every time Princes Charles landed an aeroplane with them on board. It was a scoring system, just as in *Strictly Come*

Dancing. A perfect ten. A low score would be accompanied by fake retching.

When she was living at Clarence House, Princess Elizabeth asked that the guardsmen be allowed to stand in the shade. She was greatly concerned when many soldiers fainted at a rehearsal for Trooping the Colour at Windsor.

While Prince Charles and Lady Diana were announcing their engagement to the world's press on the lawn of Buckingham Palace on 24 February 1981, two people were twitching their curtains, hoping not to be seen, in the windows behind them: the Prince's valet and the Queen.

In May 1966 Tony Benn fell into conversation with Michael Adeane, the Queen's private secretary, at a state banquet about the Labour party's new arrangements for electing their own leader, which spared the Queen the awkwardness of choosing a new prime minister/leader in the event of the sudden resignation of the previous one. 'And what would happen if you were knocked down by a bus,' Benn impertinently asked Adeane. 'Oh I think she could just about manage.'

The Duchess of Windsor always had a notepad and gilt pencil with her at dinner. The next day she would give her servants their 'notes'.

When Bobo suggested that Grenadier Guards had made off with food parcels sent to her as wedding presents, Princess Elizabeth was very cross. She would hear no wrong of the first regiment of which she had been made colonel-in-chief.

At Buckingham Palace in the 1940s, there were two Duchesses of Edinburgh. One later became the Queen. The other was a waitress in the junior staff dining room, of Scottish origin, real name Betty Burns. On account of her grand connections and wonderful clothes, she was accorded ducal status and recognised as such by all the Royal Family. The Queen, later Queen Mother, was concerned to know what she was planning to wear for Ascot. Once the 'Duchess' was supposed to be receiving her Christmas present from the King and Queen but was found to be in the bath. 'My wee Queen will wait for the Duchess,' she declared.

In the 1940s, a footman once told Princess Margaret of his undying passion for her at the Christmas Staff Ball. He was unembarrassed and retained his position.

Princess Elizabeth asked Bobo to find out from his valet, John Dean, what her husband was planning to wear to a function. 'That will be difficult,' said Bobo. 'They're not speaking.' A few days previously the Duke had called his servant a 'stupid clot'.

King George VI had a similarly rocky relationship with his valet, Jerram. Hearing her husband and John Dean arguing through the connecting door, Princess Elizabeth would say to Bobo: 'Listen to them. They're just like Papa and Jerram, only worse.'

Princess Elizabeth heard that her husband's valet's parents had come to Buckingham Palace on the day of her mother and father, the King and Queen's, silver wedding anniversary. She offered them her dressing room so they would have a decent view of the procession.

The Queen and the Duke of Edinburgh are interested in feedback. Their servants must always pass on comments overheard from the crowd, of whatever nature.

The Duke of Edinburgh's valet thought nothing of Patricia Brabourne's cottage in the village street at Mersham-le-Hatch in Kent. The front door opened straight into the dining room. It was the sort of place people dreamt of retiring to, the valet pronounced with contempt. The Duke of Edinburgh and Princess Elizabeth stayed there often.

Among the duties of the Duke of Edinburgh's valet was to feed him sandwiches while driving. This avoided delay.

The infant Prince Charles accosted his father's valet in a palace corridor: 'Those are my Papa's clothes. Where are you taking them?'

Princes Charles, in boyhood, addressed the chauffeur, Mr Pollard, as Polly. One time he asked for the radio to be switched off. 'I don't like Mrs Dale's Diary,' he explained.

At Birkhall there is only one staircase, so staff out clubbing until 4 a.m. had to creep past the royal bedrooms to get to their attic accommodation.

At Birkhall, the Duke of Edinburgh would drive over to Balmoral if a film was being shown there with Princess Elizabeth at his side and any staff who wanted to go in the back. The Princess begged him to slow down and watch out for the rabbits.

At Birkhall, John Gibson was persuaded by the Scottish soldiers guarding Balmoral Castle to try on a kilt. 'You've got to take off your underpants,' they said 'It's the regimental rules.' While they were taking photographs of him in his kilt, one of the soldiers produced a mirror – to check what was going on under the kilt. 'I can see!' he bellowed. 'He hasn't got them on.' What they didn't know what that Princess Elizabeth was on the other side of a nearby hedge, in fits of laughter. 'Did you enjoy having your photograph taken?' she asked later.

On Christmas Day 2004 an unfortunate junior foot-man, Fraser Marlton Thomas, aged twenty-five, thought the Queen was getting up from the table. But she wasn't. She sat straight back down again but not before he had removed her chair. Sprawled on the floor, luckily unhurt, the Queen was soon as amused as the rest of her family.

With the
Church

———

'What a fool! What a thing to say to the Queen,' John Andrew, an Anglican clergyman in New York, lamented. The Queen had spotted him on the corner of Park Avenue and 61st Street as she drove by during her state visit to America in 1976. 'There's John Andrew!' she called out. 'See you tonight,' the cleric had replied. But there must be some truth in the much-made claim that Church of England ordinates enjoy an especially casual relationship with the monarch. More recently, a Dean said to the Queen on parting, 'Do give my best wishes to X when you see him next.' Back in the car, the Queen said, 'Is there anyone who X does not know? I'm always being asked to convey messages to him.'

The Duke of Edinburgh drove so fast in a Bentley sports car that he reached his destination, the Archbishop's palace at York, earlier than expected which was why the Archbishop was still asleep in his chair.

Our Realms and
Interests Over
the Seas

———ᨈᨈ———

At the opening of the St Lawrence Seaway, *Britannia* was squashed absolutely tight in the Beauharnois lock. The Queen and President Eisenhower tried to push her away from the side with their own hands.

In 1979, in Africa, the Queen was so absorbed in conversation with Dr Hastings Banda, 'life president' of Malawi, she didn't notice she had her elbows on the table. This was when the Commonwealth was in turmoil over Rhodesia and the Queen was determined to calm things down.

The Queen first met George W. Bush in 1991, while on a state visit to his father. 'Are you the black sheep of the family?' she enquired.

The Queen Mother, visiting America in November 1954, was delighted with the towels in the bathroom, not only the sheer number, but the size; ranging, she said, from 'large to tiny'.

The Queen's speeches were of course, heard in respectful silence. Heads of government, attending her banquets at the Commonwealth Conference, took a different approach. 'Come on, Your Majesty,' they'd shout as she was speaking, 'do you really mean that?' She'd say: 'Do be quiet! I'm trying to make a speech!' 'They were joyous occasions,' said one onlooker.

On the American leg of the coronation tour, FBI agents were over-enthusiastic. One, disguised in a green satin evening dress, tried to follow the Queen into the ladies' room. The Hon Mary Morrison, lady-in-waiting, had to fight her off.

The Mayor of Hamburg, by tradition, refuses to descend the enormous staircase of the town hall to greet any visitor, however important. When the Queen came on a state visit in 1965, the Mayor at that time found a gracious way out of it: 'I won't go down to greet even the Queen of England, but I will go down to greet a lady.'

The Queen was greeted on her state visit to America in 1991 by a lectern almost her equal in height. She had to read her speech, but all anyone could see was 'a talking hat'. President George Bush Sr, speaking previously to welcome her, and of immense height, had forgotten his allotted task, which was to pull out a small platform for the Queen to stand on when he'd finished. His wife, Barbara, was furious with him at the lunch afterwards.

In the 1980s a dispute between Britain and France over lamb exports unfortunately coincided with the Queen Mother's private visit to Maurice Hennessy's estate near Cognac. Her treasurer, Ralph Anstruther, went out in advance to ensure that all sheep were removed from royal view.

During ten weeks of voluntary work in Patagonia in 2000, Prince William was commended for his ability to mix well with others and for his down-to-earth manner. He didn't mind at all being addressed as 'Little Princess' by fellow volunteers.

On the coronation tour, the Queen was named by Maoris, 'The Rare White Heron of the Single Flight'. Later, on board her ship, the *Gothic*, she performed the haka 'complete with grunts and exaggerated gestures…'

The Quebec premier, René Lévesque, had no wish to meet the Queen in 1977. Rather, he wanted independence for Quebec and to be rid of her as Head of State. Nevertheless, he came to a lunch given by Federal Prime Minister Pierre Trudeau. Behind his back as he was introduced to the Queen he held a lit cigarette. He continued to smoke as they spoke and wore a disobliging face. The Queen took no notice.

In April 1965, the Queen was climbing over a fence at the Badminton Horse Trials while her mother, in an orange silk duster coat and high heels was battling through a gale in the Camargue. Arriving at a bird sanctuary she was told in no uncertain terms that if she wanted to see the flamingos she'd have to get out of her car and walk. One of her party said, 'The Queen Mother had no idea the Camargue was quite such a wild and romantic place. In spite of the tempest she is delighted.'

On the coronation tour the Queen often held up her pearls when no one was looking to avoid an unfortunate tan line.

Our Wild Side

The Queen was greatly excited about Ginny Airlie's 70th birthday party at Annabel's in February 2003. She hadn't been to a nightclub, she said, since she was first married. On an engagement the following day at St Albans Abbey in Hertfordshire, the Dean asked her if she knew Robert Salisbury, also present. 'Oh yes,' she said, 'Robert and I were in a nightclub last night until half past one.'

Max Miller greeted the Queen Mother before his show. 'I've got two versions, the white and the blue. Which would you prefer?' 'I think I'll have the blue,' was the unhesitating reply.

'Are you going up to Oxford?' the Queen Mother, then Queen, enquired of the debutant daughter of Lord Longford, Antonia Pakenham, later Lady Antonia Fraser. 'Well, you must have a fling first.'

In the 1970s, Prince Charles took up windsurfing, then a novel sport frowned upon by the old guard. He confided in a friend that he liked particularly to display his prowess right in front of the Royal Yacht Squadron at Cowes and imagine the blustering disapproval of the old sea dogs within.

The Duke of Norfolk, the Earl Marshal in charge of important royal ceremonies, was approached by a peer anxious that he would not be invited to the Queen's coronation because he had been divorced. 'Good God, man,' the Duke replied, 'this is a coronation, not Royal Ascot.'

Much huff and puff at court when Tim Lawrence, a mere equerry, began a relationship with Princess Anne. But the Queen thought otherwise. 'I've decided I'm not old-fashioned enough to be Queen,' she told a supporter of the liaison.

Offered a red dress at one of her family's favourite fashion houses, Pippa Middleton said, 'Oh no. I've got to tone down.'

On 16 August 1945, the day after VJ Day, Princess Elizabeth recorded in her diary: 'Out in crowd again. Embankment, Piccadilly. Rained so fewer people. Congaed into house. Sang till 2 a.m. Bed at 3 a.m.' Intriguing that Buckingham Palace is a 'house'.

If the men lingered too long at the dinner table after the ladies had withdrawn, there was a serious risk that the Queen Mother would lead a disruptive chorus of women making sheep noises outside the dining room windows. This is what happened once when Her Majesty stayed at Uplowman in Devon with her niece, Margaret Rhodes.

'Please give me an assignment,' young Prince Harry, wearing pretend camouflage, soldier-like, asked the protection officer at Kensington Palace. 'Go and find your aunt,' the policeman commanded the small boy, knowing that this lady lived in the Palace complex. 'And here's a two-way radio, so you can inform me when the mission is complete.' This Harry did. But then there was radio silence. Where was he? Harry failed to report back from the police hut at the gate, as he had been told to do. The officer was seriously worried. At last a signal came through on the radio. There was the sound of traffic in the background. 'Where are you?' A pause while the boy Prince carried out reconnaissance. 'Outside Tower Records in the High Street.' The officer absolutely flew to fetch him back.

'I have my reputation to consider,' the Queen Mother remarked to her trusted servant, William Tallon, after he had poured her a rather small gin.

What We Like and What We Don't Like

'I don't like *The Bill*. I just can't help watching it,' the Queen told Ryan Parry in 2003, while that gentleman was posing as a footman, rather than the reporter from the *Mirror* that he actually was.

Did you know that the Queen collects pepper grinders? The artist, Frolic Weymouth, gave her one from an Italian restaurant – a plastic waiter. Turn the head for pepper and it shrieks with a joke Italian accent, 'You're breaking my neck.' The Queen was amused.

Arriving at Buckingham Palace in 1937, Princess Elizabeth established a stable for her thirty toy horses in the passage outside her bedroom. There they still were on her wedding day, ten years later.

As a child, swimming was the Queen's thing. She won the Children's Challenge Shield at London's Bath Club. She showed no skill at tennis or needlework and during the Second World War was useless at knitting.

Princess Elizabeth had a sketch of James Gunn's *Conversation Piece* of Hilaire Belloc, G.K. Chesterton and Maurice Baring hanging in her sitting room at Clarence House.

The Queen visited a modern hotel near Heathrow and the new Berkeley Hotel in Knightsbridge to get decor tips. She also bought works by Mary Fedden, James Taylor, Ivon Hitchens and Robin Darwin.

Queen Mary took her grandchildren on educational outings, including to Mount Pleasant Post Office. But in February 1956, the Queen Mother took her small grandchildren, Charles and Anne, to see an exhibition about Nigeria, while their mother was on a tour of that country. Fully expecting them to be bored to death, just as her own daughters had been when taken on improving expeditions to museums by *their* grandmother, Queen Mary. She called it 'doing a Granny'.

In the 1960s, the Queen was amused by the satirical TV show, *Beyond the Fringe* even though the establishment of which she was head was crucified. Once she viewed it accompanied by two other targets, the Foreign Secretary, the Earl of Home and the Lord Chamberlain, the Earl of Scarborough.

The Queen Mother enjoyed cookery programmes on TV, especially *Two Fat Ladies*. *Dad's Army* was another favourite, of course.

Ted Hughes wrote a poem for the Queen Mother on her 95th birthday comparing her to a six-rooted tree.

The Queen Mother's friends gave her a hut in a treasured spot on Deeside. She named it 'the Old Bull and Bush', after the Hampstead pub sealed forever in memory by the music hall song of the 1920s, which was sung by Florrie Forde.

Prince Harry's bedroom at Highgrove featured Zulu artefacts and Arsenal scarves.

In 1999, Dick Francis and his wife (the Dick Francis novels were in fact a joint effort) decided to retire from the writing life. At Cheltenham Racecourse they had an opportunity to present their last book to the Queen Mother. But they'd forgotten one thing. 'I'm so looking forward to next year,' she said, on receiving the gift. 'I always said you could dedicate a book to me when I reach a hundred and next year will be your chance.' So that was that. Retirement plans shelved, they had to scurry home and get on with another book.

A visitor to Highgrove found an intruder in her glass of beer: a goldfish. And nearby a grinning young man with red hair making a bad job of covering up his glee.

Pink carnations and roses were supplied in abundance for the farewell dinner given by the Mountbattens at Chester Street the night before the Royal Family departed for the South African Tour in 1947. Pink was the Queen's favourite colour.

At the Royal Academy in the year of her diamond jubilee, the composer, Thomas Adès was crushed that the Queen did not speak to him as she passed. But she must have seen, for she turned back and said, 'It's so important – music.'

Princess Elizabeth's favourite radio programmes were *Much Binding in the Marsh*, Tommy Handley and Wilfred Pickles. In more recent times, she has been known to watch *Countdown* with her sergeant-at-arms Paul Whybrew.

An innovation made by the Duke of Edinburgh on arrival at Buckingham Palace in 1952 was to add the *Daily Mirror* and the *Sunday Pictorial* to the newspaper order.

On a tour of Canada in 1950, the Duke of Edinburgh chased his wife down the corridor of the train, wearing some joke false teeth.

The enticing tin of nuts the Duke of Edinburgh left on his wife's desk when they were touring Canada in the 1950s turned out to be home to a plastic snake which sprang out when the tin was opened.

Prince Charles learned to water-ski by sitting on an old wooden dining chair which was dragged along by a power boat.

'Don't get me started,' said Camilla Duchess of Cornwall at Fortnum and Mason in December 2014. She was viewing needlework done by prisoners as part of a rehabilitation programme called 'Fine Cell Work.' Naturally she was asked how her own efforts compared.

Members of the public presenting flowers to the Queen Mother wrapped in newspaper or tin foil found special favour. She assumed they'd picked them themselves rather than stopped off at a garage.

'Do you exhibit internationally as well as in Margate?' the Queen asked Tracey Emin at the opening of the new gallery there in November 2011. It's hard to judge the extent to which this was a naïve question.

Who can carry on with a huge and challenging jig-saw while on her feet talking to guests? The Queen, it would seem, according to Richard Crossman who, in January 1967 at Sandringham, never once caught her looking away from her hostess duties.

At Mansion House in July 1962, the Queen led community singing of 'On Mother Kelly's Doorstep' as part of John Betjeman's picture-and-poetry story of London's history. Afterwards she told Randolph Sutton, who made his name singing the song in London's music hall between the world wars, 'I'm glad they sang the chorus. I thought perhaps they were going to be stuffy about it.' The chorus is about Nellie:

> *She'd got a little hole in her frock*
> *Hole in her shoe, hole in her sock*
> *Where her toe peeped through.*

Standing behind the bar of the Queen Vic, on a tour of the *EastEnders* studio in 2001, the Queen remarked that the set was very small. She didn't know, though, that, in those days at least, the show was not broadcast on Wednesdays. 'But Camilla's a fan,' Barbara Windsor said, looking on the bright side.

The Queen loved *Kojak*, an American police drama of the 1970s, which starred Telly Savalas.

The Queen loved crime thrillers by P.D. James, Agatha Christie and Dick Francis.

The Early Days

Princess Andrew, mother of the Duke of Edinburgh, lunched at Windsor on the day the Queen was born.

Princess Elizabeth's hair began to curl at five months owing to the expertise of her nurse, Mrs Knight, known as Allah.

The infant Princess Elizabeth greeted the seventh Earl Spencer who had ridden over to Naseby Hall in Northamptonshire, which the Duke of York was renting for hunting: 'How nice to see you! Do please come in, but you'd better leave your horse outside.'

'I shall call her Bud,' said Princess Elizabeth, when informed that her new sister was to be called 'Margaret Rose'. 'She isn't really a rose yet. She's only a bud.'

'Oh look, what a lot of people.' Princess Elizabeth was standing in the dining room window at 145 Piccadilly, her childhood home. She never understood why she attracted so much attention.

The little princesses' school day at 145 Piccadilly involved lessons from 9.30 a.m. to 11 a.m. only.

At Royal Lodge, Princess Elizabeth had a cage of blue budgies which were her own responsibility.

Lilibet was keen on Woolies for Christmas presents.

The little princesses struggled with maths. Queen Mary remarked that neither of them would ever have to do their own household accounts so the timetable was altered in favour of history.

One of Princess Elizabeth's favourite summer holiday diversions at Glamis Castle was to take the pony down to the station to watch the fish express go through.

Princess Elizabeth once poured a bottle of ink over her head because her French lessons consisted of nothing but writing out columns of verbs.

At Glamis, Princess Elizabeth and her friends liked to put pins held by chewing gum on the railway line. After the train had gone by, they had turned into scissors.

Princess Elizabeth was passing from her history lesson to her poetry lesson at the moment her uncle abdicated and she became heiress presumptive.

A Girl Guide troop was specially formed for the little princesses at Buckingham Palace. At the first meeting, the other children showed up in their best frocks and white gloves. 'How will they roll about and get dirty?' Princess Elizabeth protested. Nor were the outside children as excited as they might have been about cooking sausages. Finally there was a game where they piled up their shoes, mixed them up then tried to find them again. Some of the children did not recognise their own shoes. The little princesses couldn't believe it.

Princess Margaret, aged six, announced a major discovery: 'Dog and God are the same word changed round.'

The Queen Mother liked to dress her children alike even though they weren't twins. The practice was continued until at least 1945, when the two princesses were in identical outfits for the thanksgiving service for the end of the Second World War. Princess Elizabeth was then nineteen, and Princess Margaret fourteen.

The little princesses threw cushions at the wireless when Lord Haw-Haw was broadcasting.

What's the best way to cheer up an exiled Russian grand duchess? In 1940, the little princesses would render the Song of the Volga Boatmen if in the vicinity of the house where Grand Duchess Xenia was staying on the Balmoral estate. Luckily she never heard them.

When Princess Margaret was about five, J.M. Barrie offered her a contract for use of some of her expressions in his new play, *The Boy David*. She was to get a penny for each performance. But the work didn't run and only a small bag of coins was delivered to Buckingham Palace later. A replica of this bag resurfaced in 1997, when Princess Margaret opened the upgraded site of the Peter Pan statue in Kensington Gardens, and it was again presented to her.

Even in royal homes, the walls are thin. At Birkhall, Margaret Rhodes was kept awake by the infant Princess Margaret singing herself to sleep with 'Old

MacDonald Had a Farm'. Only after many verses with accompanying animal noises did she drop off. In later life the Princess was devoted to late-night singing when others were ready for bed.

'What's your name?' a fellow nursery school pupil asked Prince Harry. Not so easy to explain if you're royal. 'Who am I?' the infant later asked his father.

What is Ordinary
Life Like?

Princess Margaret was intrigued by the demands of Lilibet's ATS course. 'How do you stand to attention,' she asked, 'when under a bus?'

After dinner, the Queen does not lounge about chatting. A favourite pastime is reading letters from members of the public which she keeps in enormous baskets. People write to tell her that ducklings have hatched near their home, that a drain cover has not been replaced by the local authority, that they don't like the government or the monarchy and so on.

The Queen Mother's method of 'moving on'. 'I'd love to stand here talking all day, but I really must get on.' With what? Vac-ing? Dusting? Shelling peas?

Apparently a large flowerbed would have made it impossible for the Queen Mother to press her ear to the wall around Clarence House so she could hear what passers-by on the other side were saying about her. But why should she not have climbed into the flowerbed for the purpose?

As Lilibet drove to Windsor each Friday with her mother, she eagerly looked out for certain fixtures en route: the 'very old couple' always working in the garden of their small house on the Great West Road, and 'the Jolly Grocer' and 'Old Mother Newspapers'. None of these people had an inkling of the little Princess's intense interest in them.

At Christmas 2007, Prince Harry played football in southern Helmand with a ball devised from toilet roll and black gaffer tape. Then he careered about on an old motorcycle, shrieking, 'No brakes! No brakes!'

'Do stop fiddling about with that gun.' For some reason, Princess Margaret, in the butts at Balmoral, was desperate to hear all about the Butlin's Holiday Camp Prince Philip had visited at Filey, where he'd been given a cheque for the National Playing Fields Association by Mr Billy Butlin himself. But there was little to tell. The camp was well organised, the Prince informed her.

The great feature of Christmas at Sandringham was Queen Mary's visits to old estate workers in their homes.

The minute Princess Elizabeth passed her driving test during the Second World War she set off from the ATS depot at Windsor for London – by herself. When she reached the forecourt of Buckingham Palace she was greeted by furious officials.

In October 2005, it was suddenly necessary to extend the stage of the theatre at Chatsworth House in Derbyshire because otherwise the principal dancer of the Bolshoi Ballet, Alexander Volshkov, making his grand mid-air entrance, would end up in the front row of the audience. All day the joinery team were back and forth up the stairs, passing through the Orangery shop, bearing planks of wood. Visitors to the shop looked momentarily bemused. 'What was Prince William doing there?' Then, evidently, they dismissed the thought. But they were wrong. It was Prince William, on work experience.

Touring America in 1957, the Queen especially asked to see a supermarket, a phenomenon then unknown in Britain. For her, the frozen chicken pot pies were the star attraction.

Presiding at lunch in her own Clarence House, the Queen Mother said, 'Look at us. We are just ordinary people having an ordinary lunch.' Unlikely.

Our Animal Kingdom

It was remarkable that the horses pulling the carriages of the Royal Family to and from the various national celebrations in London to mark the end of the Second World War didn't shy in the face of the cheering crowds for they had spent years working on farms. But it transpired that the 'noisier wireless programmes' had been played while they worked.

'She will never see a racecourse,' was the verdict of the trainer Captain Boyd-Rochfort, on the filly, Astrakhan, in 1948. But the horse had been a wedding present from the Aga Khan and anyway Princess Elizabeth didn't give up easily. A horse physiotherapist did wonders and Astrakhan not only ran in races but won them.

'Get that dog out of my house by three o'clock,' the Queen, not often furious, said to her Private Secretary. In 1973, the wife of the President of Zaire had smuggled a 'filthy little dog' through customs and into Buckingham Palace. It could have been rabid.

In 1973, the assassin of Sir Richard Sharples, the governor-general of Bermuda, was sentenced to death but appealed in the last resort to the Queen for mercy. 'He's got a cheek asking me,' Her Majesty snapped. 'He even shot the dog.'

The Queen's gun dogs at one time were called Donna, Sherry and Gem.

'Meldrum said I was needed early.' The Queen, was always eager to muck in if the shoot is short-handed. She went around, with her dogs, picking up birds that had been shot.

Princess Elizabeth patted Big Game on a visit to Beckhampton in the 1940s. She felt it was such a privilege to touch this important horse that she didn't wash her hand for some time afterwards.

The Queen listened in to horse auctions over the phone.

Touring the Caribbean in the 1980s, the Queen had her arm in a sling. 'Did you fall off your horse?' somebody asked. 'No, the horse fell on me,' the Queen explained.

There was a pause as the going-away carriage drew up at Waterloo Station in November 1947 containing the newly married Princess Elizabeth and the Duke of Edinburgh. Then the door opened, followed by an inexplicable shower of rose petals at a low level. This was Susan, the royal corgi, disembarking.

As a young man, Prince Charles wanted to ride in the Grand National.

'I could have done with that earlier,' the Duke of Edinburgh remarked of a guardsman's gun as he left Guildhall after the lunch for the Queen's golden jubilee in 2002. 'When we arrived at St Paul's this morning, there were a couple of fat pigeons right outside.' It would have made quite a scene – the royal pair arriving in the gold coach for the service to commemorate the jubilee, followed by a brief shooting interlude.

The Queen was twelve minutes late for the Privy Council meeting at Balmoral in October 1967 because, out riding just beforehand, she was farthest from the house when her horse got a stone in its foot. Of course that was the one day when she'd forgotten her penknife with stone-removing spike.

Princess Margaret went out riding at Balmoral on a horse given to the Queen by premier of the Soviet Union, Nikolai Bulganin. It went over six bridges but refused the seventh, although it was no different from the others. Her family found her, hours later, still standing by the bridge with the horse. 'These Russian horses,' the Queen explained later, 'are very obstinate.'

Steak, poached chicken and rabbit were regularly on the menu in the royal homes, according to royal chef, Darren McGrady – for the corgis though, not the humans.

Royal Mother

The Queen was once being driven through the back streets of Chelsea when she spied a line of small boys in red shorts and yellow jumpers. One of them was her son, Prince Charles. 'I wanted to tap on the window but thought better of it,' she said.

'Mummy has promised us a baby,' Prince Charles, aged 5, informed a former sailor encountered on an outing to a farm with his grandmother the Queen Mother. He and Princess Anne, aged 3, had just met one in its pram and been entranced.

Commander Colville's press conference to announce that the Queen was expecting a baby, was held in the ballroom at Buckingham Palace. 'How did your ball go?' the Queen enquired subsequently.

Not even childbirth stood in the way of the Queen and her red boxes. Within forty-eight hours at

most she would be back on track. She once said that if she missed even one day she'd never get straight again.

'It's what we're made for': the Queen's view of child-bearing.

Elizabeth and Philip chose the name Charles because they liked it. Others were not keen because of Charles I and Charles II, not to mention, Bonnie Prince Charlie.

The Queen decided that Charles should wear normal clothes at the coronation. She wished to avoid a Little Lord Fauntleroy effect.

When a small boy, Prince Charles asked the Princess Royal, his great-aunt, to fetch down a jar of sweets from a high shelf so he could have some. Then they heard the Queen coming. They were both overcome by fear. The Princess Royal quickly reshelved the jar.

For Christmas in 1953, the Queen gave Prince Charles some mud-pie moulds and a red, white and blue glider, bought in advance at Harrods because she was to be away at Christmas on the great coronation tour. After saying goodbye to him in November, she broke down outside the nursery door.

Most of Prince Charles's and Princess Anne's toys had belonged to their mother and their aunt, Princess Elizabeth and Princess Margaret.

The Queen Mother wished to name her second daughter Anne, but George VI wouldn't have it. She had to settle for Margaret, the King's preference, which she considered a maid's name. Curious that when her turn came, the present Queen called her first daughter, Anne.

April 1962 and first-time mother, Pamela Hicks, daughter of Lord Mountbatten, was in trouble. Her baby, Edwina, began to howl at the crucial moment in her own christening and would not stop. Pamela was in need of a more experienced mother. And she had one, standing right next to her in the form of the Queen, who took the baby in her arms and pacified her at once.

At the state banquet for President Frei of Chile in July 1965, Barbara Castle was talking to the Queen on a sofa afterwards about Julius Nyerere ('Not his usual self at the Commonwealth Conference' the Queen thought), when Her Majesty was called away to the telephone. 'Poor Charles has got his O levels tomorrow. He needs reassurance,' she explained. Returning, she said, 'Aren't these exams awful?' She turned to Princess Margaret: 'You and I would never have got into university.'

Our Eye for
Detail

'I'm not going up there. It moved.' The Queen was in Charlottetown, Canada, in October 1964, about to leave for Quebec. Standing at the foot of the gangway that led to *Britannia*, she sensed that something was amiss. She was right. Within minutes the structure slipped and crashed to the ground. Mooring lines had been cast adrift too early. Lucky escape!

The Queen couldn't put her finger on it but something was wrong with the painted ceiling in the entrance hall of Marlborough House. Her instincts were right: the nine muses had been re-assembled in the wrong order after the ceiling had been moved from the Queen's House Greenwich.

Alan Lennox-Boyd, colonial secretary in the 1950s, mystified the Prime Minister, Anthony Eden, by asking him to investigate the grazing rights of Somali tribesmen as he prepared to meet the Queen. 'She won't be interested in that,' Eden said. But she was.

The Queen annotated the programme for a state visit of the King and Queen of Thailand in the 1960s, 'Tell the band leader under no circumstances to play excerpts from *The King and I*.'

The Queen was asked to read a proof of a biography of Prince Charles, then a child. She returned it promptly: 'Very gooey and sentimental but quite nice. There are four inaccuracies.' She gave the page numbers.

Looking at the horses in the paddock before a big race at Ascot, neither the Queen nor her racing assistant had a race card. The Queen admired a horse that subsequently appeared to win the race. But when the assistant commented on this, she said, 'Oh no. The winner had one of those awful white plastic bridles.' She'd noted this detail in a trice as the horses thundered past.

Princess Elizabeth saw at the Royal Academy in 1939 a painting by A.K. Lawrence, 'Queen Elizabeth Visits her Army at Tilbury'. Visiting an Essex town hall where it hung twenty-six years later, she recognised it at once.

Princess Margaret, overwrought in 1974 for various reasons, telephoned a friend proposing to jump out of the window if that person didn't come over at once. The friend called the Queen who said, 'Don't worry. Her bedroom is on the ground floor.'

'Can't he have his OBE back?' Peter O'Sullivan, the racing commentator, decided to intercede on behalf of Lester Piggott, who'd been incarcerated for tax evasion. In the view of many there were mitigating circumstances. 'Look here,' said the Queen, 'he's not only been naughty, he's been stupid.' Piggott had sent the Inland Revenue a cheque from an account whose existence he'd concealed from them.

'I would have thought civil servants do what they're told,' the Queen remarked to Richard Crossman in January 1967. 'I'm afraid that's not true,' he replied. 'How do you know?' she said. Crossman explained his own experience of an especially obstructive (in his view) permanent secretary, Dame Evelyn Sharp.

Queen Mary's christening gift to Prince Charles: '…a silver-gilt cup and cover which George III had given to a godson in 1780. So I gave a present from my grt-grandfather to my grt-grandson 168 years later…' This kind of thing greatly appealed to Queen Mary.

'Are red socks allowed now?' the Queen asked a Welsh Guards officer at dinner. Earlier in the day she had seen out of the window a Welsh Guards soldier erecting a bandstand at Windsor. Why weren't his socks green?

'What is unique about this regiment?' the Duke of Edinburgh enquired at a dinner of the Welsh Guards, already knowing the answer. 'It is the only one in which the colonel is legally married to the colonel-in-chief.'

Cost Cutting

At Christmas 1953, the Queen Mother, only recently widowed, found herself relegated to Queen Mary's room at Sandringham because of an excess of visitors. But conditions were primitive owing to Her Late Majesty Queen Mary being set against radiators. George VI had had pipes laid but no more. There were also no power points and no fixed basin.

Once at Windsor the Queen looked out from her private apartments at bedtime and saw that all the lights were on in the public part of the castle. With her master of the household she set out to switch them off. It was a terrible struggle because of newfangled light switches that could be switched off but came back on again for no good reason. But, finally, darkness was achieved. The last hurdle was getting back again – in the dark.

Economies at Sandringham in the 1970s meant no more tray service to bedrooms – apparently. Nobody could imagine the impact when Princess Margaret and Bobo MacDonald, the Queen's dresser, arrived, which was the resumption of tray service.

On Nevis in 1993, Prince Harry organised a Giant Toad Derby. He encouraged the adults to place bets and, as owner of the winning toad, raked in good dollars.

No wonder the Queen is always careful with money. Her relations have always been so expensive. 'What with my mother and her castles and my mother-in-law and her nunneries…' she once said.

Prince Philip wouldn't throw anything away. He kept a suit of his father's even though it had been darned and was moth-eaten.

Clarence House was shut down for the summer holidays when the Duke of Edinburgh returned unexpectedly from Balmoral. 'Run up the road and get some fish and chips,' he instructed his valet. But the nearest chippie was in Edgware Road. So they telephoned to Prunier, a nearby luxe restaurant, instead.

The aircraft bearing the foreign secretary and the Prince of Wales back from the funeral of King Hassan of Morocco in 1999 stopped for refuelling in Portugal. But the RAF credit card was refused and a whip round had to be organised on board to pay for the fuel.

In America in 1957, the Queen toured Washington DC's National Gallery of Art. 'I'd liked to have bought a Monet that was for sale in London,' she told the director, John Walker, 'but I couldn't afford it.'

'This is one of Granny's bargains,' the Queen often says, when showing a needlework self-portrait by the eighteenth-century Mary Knowles acquired by Queen Mary in Bond Street.

Ladies and
Gentlemen of
the Press

At his stag night, the Duke of Edinburgh, assisted by his uncle, Lord Mountbatten, persuaded the photographers to swap roles. The royalties would take pictures of the pressmen – with their cameras. But it was a trick. As soon as the equipment was in their hands, they smashed it up.

Ray Bellisario, the original paparazzo, played cat and mouse with the Royal Family in the 1960s and 1970s. He took long-lens photographs of Princess Alexandra on honeymoon at Birkhall from the public road and caught the Queen walking in the gardens of Buckingham Palace with the Duke of Windsor from the nearby Hilton Hotel. But the Queen was eager to meet him. 'I've seen you so many times and in so many places,' she said. This approach was disconcerting to say the least. 'You must travel as much as we do.'

In Amsterdam once, in the 1960s, the Queen's car was stuck in traffic. Her detective, Albert Perkins, was busy trying to shoo photographers away. But the Queen had a better idea. She put on what she later called her 'Miss Piggy face'. None of the pictures were usable.

Walking near Balmoral with a friend, Princess Margaret came across a photographer who regularly followed her. There happened to be an AA man nearby. 'Cover me, will you?' the Princess commanded. But he misunderstood and covered his own face.

'Television,' the Duke of Edinburgh confided in Tony Benn in 1968, 'kills all ceremonial.' 'Yes,' Benn replied, 'that's why Bessie Braddock refuses to appear on TV.' The Duke was evidently not impressed by the comparison of his wife with Bessie Braddock.

'Arthur, I see you're wearing your really horrible green coat again,' Prince William called out to Arthur Edwards, the *Sun* photographer, during a photocall on the ski slopes in March 2005. 'Now don't be rude. That's unfair,' his father instructed.

On Wednesday 2 October 1968, the front page of the *Daily Express* carried a huge photograph of the Queen holding a newly born Prince Edward, surrounded by her other children and husband. Only Princess Anne was missing. The unusual feature of the photo was that it had been taken in the Queen's bedroom some four years before and the Queen is actually in bed, holding the baby. There is much splendour and drapery but even so, this was going too far. The *Express* promised days and days of such photos but the palace put a stop to it at once.

Within the
Family

The Prince of Wales planned to hold a charity dinner (substantial American cheques a possibility) at Hampton Court Palace on 22 June 2000. But it was already booked! Fortunately the Queen was at Windsor that week for Ascot, so Buckingham Palace was free. Thus Camilla made her first visit there as 'out' consort. 'When the cat's away, the mice will play,' the Prince remarked in his speech at the dinner, adding that it was not often that he was allowed to use the palace.

Queen Mary made the King and Lilibet pick ivy off the walls of Sandringham. Their hands were so poisoned they had to take a trip to Eastbourne to recover.

For Christmas 2011, the Duchess of Cambridge gave Prince Harry a plastic grow-your-own girlfriend.

Agnes Warfield led the State Department team responsible for the American side of organising the Queen's state visit to that country in 1991. Familiar? Who was a certain unmentionable person before she was Spencer, Simpson and finally Windsor?

Arriving at Clarence House to have tea with her granddaughter, Queen Mary would say, 'Any good new jokes today, Lilibet? You must tell me the latest.'

Princes Charles, aged five, went on board an aircraft in Scotland to greet his grandmother, the Queen Mother. They were just about to disembark together when – where were his sweets? He'd left them behind. 'You wait there, Granny,' he said.

For Christmas 1937, one year after the abdication of Edward VIII, the Queen Mother, then Queen, sent the exiled Duke of Windsor a set of antique dessert knives and forks with porcelain handles. Subsequently she always sent him a Christmas card, although they were found heaped in his bath after the Duchess's death.

'You look just like your father,' pensioner Norma Wood told Prince William on a visit to Sighthill, an impoverished Glasgow housing estate in September 2001. 'Oh, don't say that. I can't bear it,' the Prince replied.

'Are you keeping up? It's quite a quick game,' Prince William called out to his father during a charity polo match in 2003. 'We'll get the stabilisers out and put them on your horse.' Prince Charles made a suitably dignified response. 'Don't worry. I'm just making a nuisance of myself,' Prince William assured him. 'That's not too difficult,' flashed Prince Charles. 'Well, it's hereditary,' returned Prince William. Their banter must have been equal to their play for they won the match.

When Prince William claimed credit for setting up the goals in a polo match in 2003 although he did not score any, Prince Harry said, 'Shut up! I nearly fell off my horse trying to get you to hit the ball and you missed it, spoon.' Prince Charles, who was present, took a while to catch on. 'Spoon, did you say?' 'Spoon, it's not a swear word,' Prince Harry replied. 'I do hope it isn't,' said his father.

'Look, Pops, they've got cherry brandy,' Prince William pointed out at Anglesey Food Fair in 2003. Some forty years before, his father had ordered cherry brandy in a pub near Gordonstoun and got into trouble for underage drinking. But as he later explained, he'd only gone into the pub to avoid photographers and thought it would be rude not to order anything. Cherry brandy was the only drink he'd ever heard of.

At a nature reserve in Botswana in 2010, staff suggested naming a baby python and a common brown house snake after Princes William and Harry who were visiting. William took charge: 'Big brother gets the python, little brother gets the common brown. It's the same colour as your hair.'

Prince Charles couldn't quite hear what a cockney voice in the crowd had said as he drove with his mother in an open landau up the course at Ascot. But the Queen had. 'Gizza wave, Liz.' She did a perfect impression for him.

House and
Garden

Every Monday, a junior gardener at Buckingham Palace picked a posy, showing the highlights of the garden at that moment, for the Queen's desk. But once he forgot. The garden team were having a meeting in their hut later in the morning when suddenly there was a presence at the back. The Queen looked directly at the young man then went away.

A former gardener reported that there were often differences of opinion as to what plants would 'do' where in the gardens at Buckingham Palace and Clarence House. Quite often the Queen and the Queen Mother were out with their spades in person, pressing on with their plans regardless.

Princess Elizabeth helped mix the green paint for the dining room at Clarence House herself. Later someone said, 'This room smells of paint.' She said, 'Put a bucket of hay in there and that'll take it away.'

No sooner was Diana engaged to the Prince of Wales in 1981 than she ruined the parquet in the Music Room at Buckingham Palace: tap-dancing lessons.

After a Privy Council meeting at Windsor in March 1967, the Queen talked about a new weedkiller called Paraquat, gesturing out of the window to a field where it was killing a lot of weeds. This particular chemical was one of the first to be banned some time later.

'I'm sure I told the gardener I don't care for variegated hostas,' the Queen remarked as she inspected the memorial in Windsor Great Park to Patrick Plunket, her much-missed deputy master of the household, who died in 1975.

The Queen Mother placed a large order for plants with a company which subsequently became a leading online supplier. When the delivery arrived, she was present and took such a liking to the employee supervising the unloading of the plants that she poached her on the spot.

Sources

Barry, Stephen. *Royal Service*, Macmillan, 1983

Bedell Smith, Sally. *Elizabeth the Queen*, Penguin, 2012

Bellisario, Ray. *To Tread on Royal Toes*, Impulse Books, 1972

Benn, Tony. *Diaries*, Arrow, 1987 to 2007

Bradford, Sarah. *Elizabeth*, Penguin, 1996

Brown, Craig, and Cunliffe, Lesley. *The Book of Royal Lists*, Sphere, 1983

Carroll, Valerie. *From Belfast's Sandy Row to Buckingham Palace*, The Mercier Press, 1994

Castle, Barbara. *The Castle Diaries 1964–70*, Weidenfeld & Nicolson, 1984

Cathcart, Helen. *Her Majesty*, W. H. Allen, 1962

Cathcart, Helen. *The Queen Mother Herself*, Hamlyn, 1979

Cathcart, Helen. *The Married Life of the Queen*, W. H. Allen, 1971

Cathcart, Helen. *The Queen Herself*, Star, 1982

Cowper-Coles, Sherard. *Ever the Diplomat*, HarperPress, 2012

Crossman, R.H.S. *Diaries*, Hamish Hamilton, 1979

Dean, John. *HRH the Duke of Edinburgh, a Portrait by his Valet*, Hale, 1954

Holden, Anthony. *The Queen Mother*, Sphere, 1985

Hutchins, Chris. *Harry The People's Prince*, The Robson Press, 2013

Mullins, Chris. *A View from the Foothills*, Profile Books, 2010

Parker, Michael. *It's All Going Terribly Wrong: The Accidental Showman*, Bene Factum Publishing, 2012

Quinn, Tom. *Backstairs Billy, The Life of William Tallon, the Queen Mother's Most Devoted Servant*, The Robson Press, 2015

Rhodes, Margaret. *The Final Curtsey*, Birlinn Ltd and Umbria Press, 2012

Robinson, Christine. *Chatsworth, the Housekeeper's Tale*, Bannister Publications, 2014

Shawcross, William. *The Selected Letters of Queen Elizabeth the Queen Mother*, Macmillan, 2012

Shawcross, William. *Queen Elizabeth the Queen Mother, The Official Biography*, Macmillan 2009

Turner, Graham. *Elizabeth the Woman and the Queen*, Macmillan and Telegraph Books, 2002

Tyrrel, Rebecca. *Camilla, an Intimate Portrait*, Short Books, 2004

I am most grateful for the help of Thomas Adès, Alan Hollinghurst, Ian Jefferis, Benedict Jenks, Wesley Kerr, John McEntee, Peter Parker, Gabrielle de Wardener, and many, many others.